THE ROAD TO WAR

BY JOHN HAMILTON

VISIT US AT
WWW.ABDOPUBLISHING.COM

Published by ABDO Publishing Company, PO Box 398166, Minneapolis, MN 55439.
Copyright ©2013 by Abdo Consulting Group, Inc. International copyrights reserved in all countries. No part of this book may be reproduced in any form without written permission from the publisher. ABDO & Daughters™ is a trademark and logo of ABDO Publishing Company.

Printed in the United States of America, North Mankato, Minnesota.
112012
012013

 PRINTED ON RECYCLED PAPER

Editor: Sue Hamilton
Graphic Design: John Hamilton
Cover Design: Neil Klinepier
Cover: Painting by Don Troiani, www.historicalartprints.com
Interior Photos and Illustrations: AP Images, p. 12, 16, 25; Corbis, p. 5, 9, 19, 22, 23; Getty Images, p. 1, 10-11, 13, 17, 20-21, 22; John Hamilton, p. 7, 15, 24, 28; Military and Historical Image Bank, p. 26, 27; National Park Service (base map), p. 28; Thinkstock, p. 3, 4, 6, 8, 14, 28.

ABDO Booklinks
To learn more about the American Revolution, visit ABDO Publishing Company online. Web sites about the American Revolution are featured on our Book Links pages. These links are routinely monitored and updated to provide the most current information available. Web site: www.abdopublishing.com

Library of Congress Control Number: 2012914138

Cataloging-in-Publication Data

Hamilton, John.
 The American Revolution: the road to war / John Hamilton.
  p. cm. — (American Revolution)
Includes index.
ISBN 978-1-61783-678-7
1. United States—History—Revolution, 1775-1783—Campaigns—Juvenile literature. I. Title.
973.3—dc22

2012914138

OCTOBER 2013

CONTENTS

THE SEEDS OF REBELLION

Great Britain's King George III took the throne in October 1760. He was just 22 years old. There was much fanfare, both at home and in Great Britain's American colonies. People were optimistic that the young king would find new and better ways of governing his colonial subjects.

In 1763, Great Britain won a long war against old enemies, including France. American colonists hoped the new peace would result in prosperity and stability. On the surface, things seemed to be going well for the colonies. For the most part, they were left alone to govern themselves. They were proud members of the British Empire, eager to build happy lives in the New World, and to make a profit doing so.

But by 1775, colonists were noisily demanding independence from Great Britain. What had happened in those few short years? How could their lives have changed so much that they now desired freedom from their mother country?

King George III

4

By 1775, the British colonies in America were in full rebellion.

Great Britain's 13 American colonies were divided into three regions, all located next to the Atlantic Ocean: New England in the northeast, the Middle Colonies, and the Southern Colonies.

The New England colonies included Massachusetts, Connecticut, Rhode Island, and New Hampshire. Their most productive industries included farming, fishing, shipping, lumber, and shipbuilding. There were also many small business owners, such as printers, carpenters, and tailors. Major seaports included Boston, Massachusetts, and Newport, Rhode Island.

The Middle Colonies included New York, New Jersey, Pennsylvania, and Delaware. There were many small farms in this region. The biggest cities were New York City and Philadelphia, Pennsylvania. New York City was one of the busiest seaports in the British Empire. The bustling city of Philadelphia was a center for culture and government.

Great Britain's Southern Colonies included Maryland, Virginia, North Carolina, South Carolina, and Georgia. They were filled with small farms, but their main source of income was from large plantations. Thousands of African American slaves worked the fields. Charleston, South Carolina, and Baltimore, Maryland, were the Southern Colonies' biggest port cities.

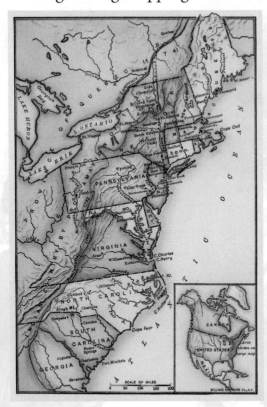

The 13 colonies at the outbreak of the American Revolution.

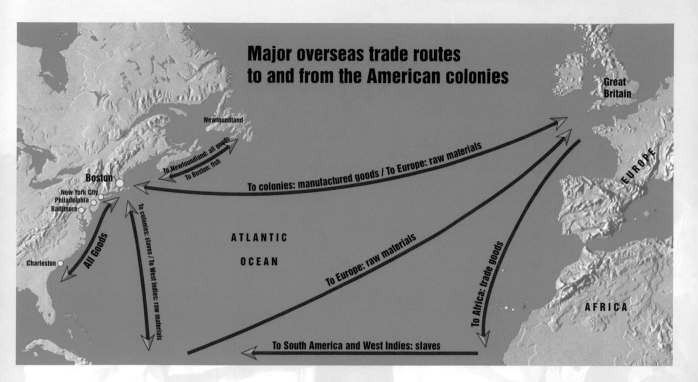

Major overseas trade routes to and from the American colonies

Great Britain

Newfoundland

To Newfoundland: all goods
To Boston: fish

Boston

New York City
Philadelphia
Baltimore

To colonies: manufactured goods / To Europe: raw materials

EUROPE

Charleston

All Goods

To colonies: slaves / To West Indies: raw materials

ATLANTIC

OCEAN

To Europe: raw materials

To Africa: trade goods

AFRICA

To South America and West Indies: slaves

The colonies were a source of tremendous profit for Great Britain. Raw materials, such as rice, sugar, molasses, indigo, and tobacco were shipped to Great Britain. In turn, manufactured British goods were bought by the colonists. This profitable system of trading was called mercantilism.

The upper classes of society were greatly enriched by mercantilism. A huge middle class also grew to support all the jobs necessary for trade, including shipping, dockworkers, and small retailers.

In 1700, the population of the American colonies was about 250,000. By 1770, that number skyrocketed to more than 2.1 million colonists. (About 450,000 of these people were African slaves, concentrated mainly in the Southern Colonies.)

Trading centers such as New York City, Philadelphia, Pennsylvania, and Boston, Massachusetts, boomed. Farm areas grew and expanded west, but most people lived within 50 miles (80 km) of the Atlantic Ocean.

The American colonies were a transplanted society. Most of the people were British. They left their familiar homes and traveled to far-flung outposts across the Atlantic Ocean. The king appointed a governor for each colony. But male, property-owning citizens elected lawmakers to form colonial legislatures. Long before the Declaration of Independence in 1776, American citizens were practicing forms of limited self-government. They were used to making their own rules and laws that were uniquely American.

Most colonists came to the colonies to start new lives. Some came to make money, or find new opportunities. Many came because they wanted to worship in their own way without fear of punishment. Different religious groups existed side-by-side in the colonies, including Quakers, Catholics, and Puritans. Observing religious freedom was another way the colonists practiced self-government.

Over time, the colonists changed. They formed their own identities and culture. After several generations, they grew to be less British. American resentment rose as Britain continued to treat its American colonies as an economic interest, a far-away land that existed just to make money.

Left: Philadelphia's Independence Hall was first known as the State House, the place where the Pennsylvania colonial government met to do its business.

Left: Mount Vernon, George Washington's Virginia home and plantation. By the 1770s, many colonists were ready for independence from Great Britain.

The system of mercantilism was beginning to break down. Because of America's remoteness from Great Britain, it took weeks, or months, to send messages back and forth across the ocean. American grievances were difficult to communicate to King George III and Parliament. In the years leading up to war, the biggest complaint was local control versus "distant authority." Americans wanted to control their own affairs, or at least have a voice in British Parliament. "No taxation without representation" was a rallying cry heard throughout the colonies.

From the British point of view, the colonists simply needed to be policed to make them obey the law, or punished to bring them back under full control. But the more Great Britain tightened its grip, the more independent minded the colonists became.

By the 1770s, the colonies were ready to cut their ties with Great Britain. The American Revolution was a change that would shake the halls of power around the world. But America's freedom would come at a cost. King George III and Parliament were determined not to give up without a fight.

The French and Indian War

The Seven Years' War raged from 1756-1763. Many European countries were involved. Great Britain and France were two of the major combatants. The armies of Prussia, Portugal, Austria, Russia, Spain, and Sweden also fought. Many of these countries, especially Great Britain and France, were long-time enemies. As their empires grew, their interests overlapped and caused conflicts. When war broke out, battles were fought in many places around the world, on land and at sea. By the time the long, bloody war ended in 1763, about one million people had been killed.

In North America, the conflict between the British and French was called the French and Indian War. It started as a regional conflict in 1754, and was later absorbed into the larger worldwide war. When the fighting started, Great Britain controlled most of the eastern coast of North America with its 13 colonies. French forces controlled

New France. This area encompassed a large swath of today's eastern Canada, including along the Saint Lawrence River, a vital waterway. It also spread southward to the Gulf of Mexico, covering most of the Ohio and Mississippi River basins. French control of these territories threatened the American colonies. It limited westward expansion and restricted trade routes.

During the French and Indian War, French forces and their Native American allies were pitted against British and colonial troops together with *their* Native American allies. Native tribes friendly to the French included the Algonquin, Ojibwa, Ottawa, and Shawnee. British and colonial forces had help from the Iroquois Confederacy and Cherokee tribes.

A battle scene from the French and Indian War in North America, which was part of a larger worldwide conflict called the Seven Years' War.

Above: A map showing the extent of New France (in green), stretching from the Saint Lawence River in the north to the Gulf of Mexico.

The French and Indian War brought European-style warfare to North America. Thousands of soldiers fought each other. At first, the French won many battles. But then British forces began capturing French strongholds.

In September 1759, British troops commanded by General James Wolfe stormed a seemingly impregnable stronghold near Quebec City, on a tall bluff overlooking the Saint Lawrence River. Wolfe and the opposing French commander were both killed in the attack, but the victorious British captured the important overlook. By 1760, most fighting ceased in North America.

In the 1763 Treaty of Paris, France surrendered most of its territory in North America. New France west of the Mississippi River, called Louisiana, was given to Spain. Canada became Britain's newest colony, and the rest of New France east of the Mississippi River was transferred to British control.

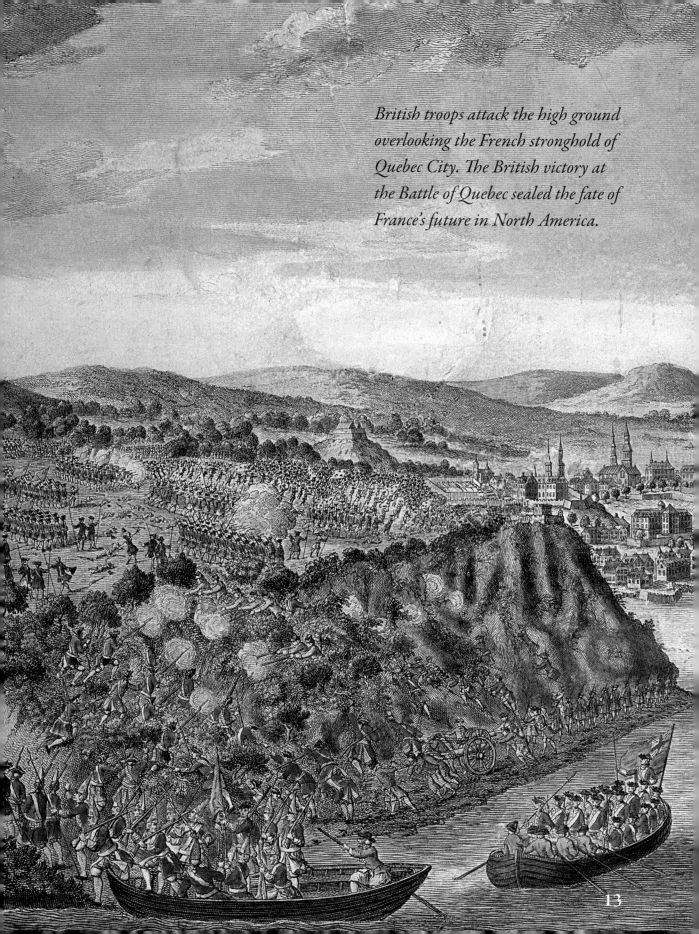

British troops attack the high ground overlooking the French stronghold of Quebec City. The British victory at the Battle of Quebec sealed the fate of France's future in North America.

13

Great Britain's victory in the global war had come at a great cost. By sending armies to fight in so many countries around the world, including North America, Africa, and India, the British government nearly went bankrupt. It thought of its colonies as an investment that would pay off handsomely over time, but for now the British treasury was bleeding money. King George III had to do two things quickly: cut expenses, and raise money.

In an attempt to cut expenses, King George III issued the Royal Proclamation of 1763. It forbade American colonists from settling west of the Appalachian Mountains. The area of land that was newly won from the French was huge. The British king knew he couldn't afford to send enough soldiers to protect colonists from Native Americans, who would fight to keep settlers off their land. He hoped the new law would keep the Native Americans peaceful. The last thing he wanted was a series of Indian uprisings. For now, the colonists would have to be content with their current boundaries.

The American colonists hated the new law. They had fought long and hard during the French and Indian War for the right to settle into new lands. They thought the king was being unfair. But if the colonists were upset about the Proclamation of 1763, they would soon be positively enraged over the king's next plan. New taxes to raise money were coming, and they would lead to open rebellion against the British Empire.

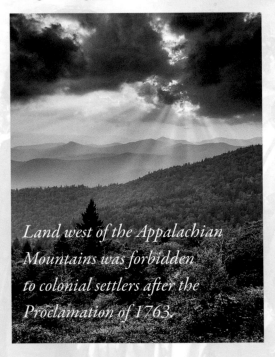

Land west of the Appalachian Mountains was forbidden to colonial settlers after the Proclamation of 1763.

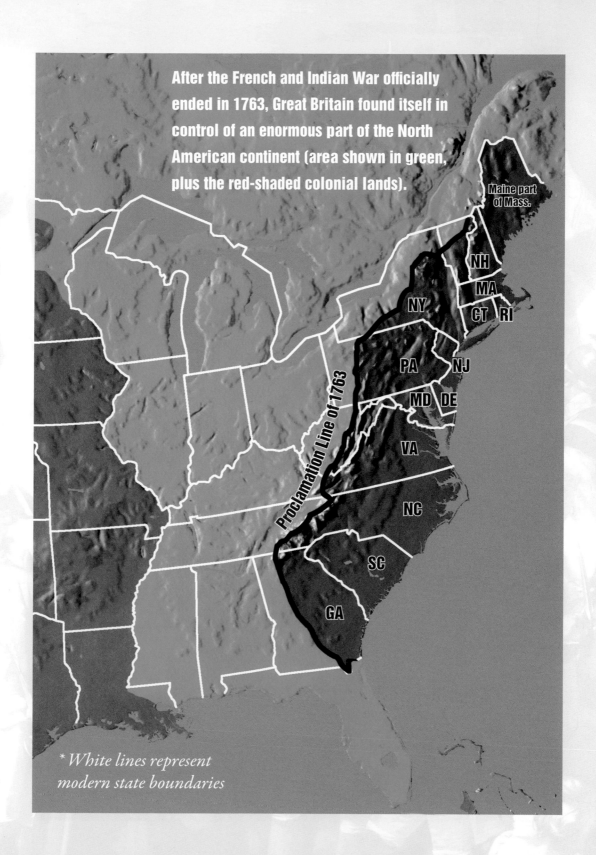

After the French and Indian War officially ended in 1763, Great Britain found itself in control of an enormous part of the North American continent (area shown in green, plus the red-shaded colonial lands).

Maine part of Mass.

NH

MA

NY

CT RI

PA

NJ

MD DE

Proclamation Line of 1763

VA

NC

SC

GA

* *White lines represent modern state boundaries*

UNFAIR TAXES

British tax stamps

It seemed like such a little thing, a few taxes to help pay for the French and Indian War. From the British point of view, the American colonies received all the benefits of being part of the British Empire. But armies and navies for protection were expensive, and the colonies weren't paying their fair share.

The British Parliament demanded that the colonists pay several new taxes. These included the Sugar Act of 1764, the Stamp Act of 1765, and the Townshend Acts of 1767. Little did King George III and Parliament realize just how enraged these taxes would make the colonists.

A riot erupts in Boston, Massachusetts, over the British Stamp Act.

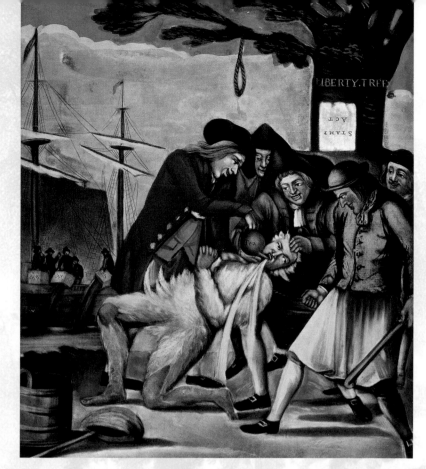

A British customs official is tarred and feathered by an angry mob in Boston, Massachusetts. This brutal practice often led to the death of the victim.

The new taxes increased the cost of everyday goods like sugar, tea, glass, and printed documents. More than the taxes themselves, the colonists objected to a distant authority (Great Britain) having the right to affect their daily lives in such a harmful way.

This was especially true because the colonies had no representatives in Parliament. They claimed that only the 13 colonial legislatures had the right to tax themselves. Therefore, the colonists said, the new taxes were illegal. "No taxation without representation" became a rallying cry throughout the colonies.

Radical groups arose such as the Sons of Liberty. This group of Patriots, who included firebrand Samuel Adams from Massachusetts, began talk of independence. Resistance was especially great in New England, including the port city of Boston. Tax collectors sent from Britain were attacked, and many were tarred and feathered.

THE BOSTON MASSACRE

By 1770, only about one-third of the colonists considered themselves "Patriots" who wanted independence. Another third were "Tories" who wanted to keep ties with Great Britain. Another third were undecided.

Alarmed at the widespread protests in the streets of Boston, the British government sent 4,000 troops, called Redcoats (or "lobsterbacks" by the colonists), to keep the peace and punish the rebellious Bostonians. But like the new taxes, these tactics backfired badly on the British.

Tired of the soldiers patrolling their streets, the citizens of Boston grew more unruly. On March 5, 1770, their anger turned to violence. A taunting mob of protesters surrounded a group of soldiers near a customs house on King Street. The mob began throwing stones and snowballs at the Redcoats. Confusion reigned. Suddenly, a flash of powder filled the air as a volley of muskets was fired into the crowd. When the smoke cleared, three colonists lay dead. Crispus Attucks, an African American, was among the first to die. Many others were hurt. Two of the injured would later die of their wounds.

The incident became known as the Boston Massacre. A jury later cleared the soldiers of murder charges, but the tragedy persuaded many colonists to support the Patriot cause.

British troops fire on an angry mob during the Boston Massacre.

19

The Boston Tea Party

By 1773, most of Great Britain's taxes on the colonies had been canceled, thanks to effective protests and negotiations. One tax remained: the tax on tea. King George III wanted to cement Britain's right to tax the colonies. He also wanted to help the cash-strapped East India Company, the British corporation that traded and shipped goods from India to Britain to the American colonies.

The East India Company was the only company that was allowed to sell tea in the colonies. The Americans got around this monopoly by buying tea smuggled from other countries. However, by passing the Tea Act of 1773, Parliament reduced import taxes normally paid by the East India Company. This actually made British tea cheaper than the smuggled tea.

Since tea would be cheaper, why were so many colonists upset? Many American colonists thought the East India Company's monopoly on tea was another step toward oppression. The Tea Act was a set of rules handed down by an uncaring British government. Americans did not trust Parliament. Many thought the tea tax and monopoly would only lead to worse situations. What was there to keep Great Britain from creating other monopolies and destroying colonial businesses?

On the night of December 16, 1773, three ships full of British tea were docked in Boston Harbor. About 60 men, some disguised as Native Americans, boarded the ships. They used hatchets to break open 342 chests of tea. Then they dumped the contents, all 9,000 pounds (4,082 kg) of it, into the water. The protest would later become known as the Boston Tea Party. Britain's overreaction to this act of defiance would be another step on the road to war.

Colonial protesters tossing British tea into Boston Harbor on December 16, 1773.

THE INTOLERABLE ACTS

The destruction of the tea in Boston outraged King George III. In 1774 Britain passed new regulations to punish the American radicals. The rules were called the Coercive Acts. (Coercing is forcing a person to do something by force or threats, like bullying.) In the colonies, the Coercive Acts were called the Intolerable Acts.

First, Boston Harbor would be closed until the East India Company was repaid for the loss of its tea. This was a heavy blow. Much business depended on ships using the busy seaport.

Above: British warships in Boston Harbor, an engraving by Paul Revere.
Right: A reenactor dressed as a British officer.

The Coercive Acts also limited the right of people in Massachusetts to govern themselves. Orders were given to arrest members of the Sons of Liberty, including Samuel Adams (although he was not captured). Boston residents were also forced to house British soldiers in their own homes. This "Quartering Act" was especially hated.

The Coercive Acts were designed to punish Boston and be a warning to the other colonies. But instead of making the colonies afraid to disobey, the unjust rules united the colonists against Great Britain.

The other colonies sent food, money, and supplies to help the suffering people of Massachusetts. On September 5, 1774, the representatives of 12 colonies met in Carpenters' Hall in Philadelphia, Pennsylvania, to form the First Continental Congress (Georgia elected not to attend). The representatives talked about how to respond to the Coercive Acts, including boycotting British goods. The Congress also wrote a direct petition to the British Parliament

Above: Attorney Patrick Henry giving an impassioned speech before the Virginia House of Burgesses.

and King George III, asking them to repeal the Coersive Acts.

Many people believed independence from Great Britain, by force of arms if necessary, was the only option. On March 23, 1775, attorney Patrick Henry addressed the Virginia House of Burgesses. In a fiery speech, Henry declared that the time for war was already upon the colonies. "I know not what course others may take," Henry said, "but as for me, give me liberty or give me death!"

THE BATTLES OF LEXINGTON AND CONCORD

During the British military occupation of Boston, Massachusetts, many people in the American colonies began to arm themselves. Gunsmiths started producing muskets and ammunition in great numbers. Weapons and gunpowder were secretly stored in houses and farms in rural areas.

A blacksmith at Colonial Williamsburg, Virginia.

In Massachusetts, groups of citizen-soldiers trained in military tactics. They called themselves the Minutemen. They pledged to be ready to fight at a moment's notice if the British continued oppressing the colonists' freedom.

War had been brewing for years in the colonies. On April 19, 1775, open rebellion finally broke out. The first military engagements of the American Revolution were the Battles of Lexington and Concord, in Massachusetts. On a country road that stretched west of Boston, 3,500 Minutemen and militia from neighboring communities fought a force of about 1,700 Redcoats.

The night before, British General and Massachusetts Royal Governor Thomas Gage ordered his troops to secretly march into the surrounding countryside and seize any Patriot weapons they could find. Rumors said that rebel weapons were being stockpiled and hidden in the nearby town of Concord. The expedition was commanded by Lt. Col. Francis Smith, who was also ordered to be on the lookout for fugitive Patriot leaders, including Samuel Adams, Dr. Joseph Warren, and John Hancock. The British commanders felt they had little to fear from the American militiamen. They considered the enemy to be mere rabble, undisciplined and unskilled in warfare.

The British mission was supposed to be secret, but Patriot spies soon warned the colonists of the plan. Couriers Paul Revere and William Dawes rode west to warn Adams, Hancock, and others that the Redcoats were coming.

Paul Revere rides through the Massachusetts countryside, warning citizens of the arrival of British troops.

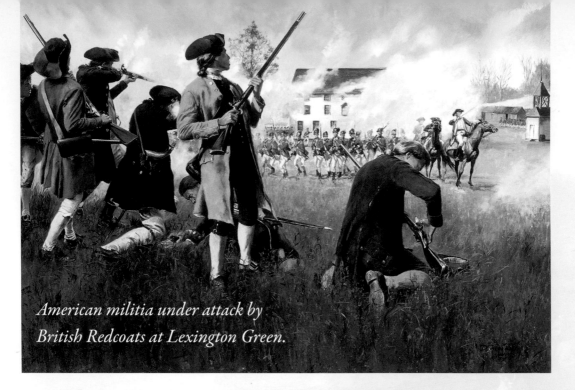

American militia under attack by British Redcoats at Lexington Green.

The British faced delays in their mission. It wasn't until the next morning, April 19, that they finally marched into the town of Lexington, about halfway to their goal of Concord. Facing them on a flat area of ground called Lexington Green was a group of 77 militiamen led by Captain John Parker. Because he was outnumbered, Parker didn't order his men to attack, but he wanted to display the Patriots' resolve. He ordered his men to stand in defiance.

British Major John Pitcairn shouted, "Disperse, ye rebels!" Slowly, the militiamen obeyed Pitcairn's order. But then a shot rang out. Nobody is sure which side fired first, but soon the British troops began firing at will at the Patriots. When the smoke cleared, eight Massachusetts men were dead. News of the skirmish quickly spread to neighboring towns.

The British troops marched on to Concord, where they conducted house-to-house searches for illegal weapons. They began burning confiscated military supplies. Meanwhile, Minutemen were pouring in from the surrounding area. By midday, thousands of armed Patriots surrounded the town.

They saw smoke rising into the air and feared the British were torching the town. Tension mounted on both sides.

At Concord's North Bridge, a group of Redcoats fired a volley at the Americans on the opposite bank of the Concord River. Concord's Major John Buttrick ordered the Minutemen to shoot back: "Fire, fellow soldiers, for God's sake fire!" For the first time in the conflict, an organized group of American colonial troops were ordered to fire at British soldiers.

Several of the Redcoats at North Bridge were killed or wounded, including three officers. The British troops panicked and pulled back, rejoining the main force. Then the British began a long, bloody retreat back to Boston, more than 20 miles (32 km) away.

For the rest of the day, the outnumbered British troops fought a running battle as they hurried back down the road. Everywhere they turned, they were shot at by thousands of angry and armed American militiamen.

Minutemen fire on British troops at Concord's North Bridge.

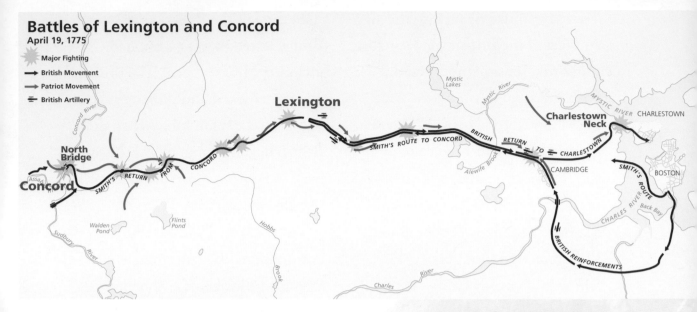

Battles of Lexington and Concord
April 19, 1775

* Major Fighting
→ British Movement
→ Patriot Movement
≡ British Artillery

At Lexington, the British were met by British reinforcements, which included artillery. The cannons gave them covering fire, which saved them from being totally wiped out before they could make it back to Boston.

By nightfall, the British staggered back into the city. They had suffered 73 dead and 200 wounded or missing. The Americans counted 49 dead and 45 wounded or missing.

The next morning the British found themselves surrounded by more than 7,000 militiamen from Massachusetts and other colonies. Boston was under siege. The Minutemen had fought well and were now on the offensive. The British were in shock. They had underestimated the Patriots' will to fight for freedom. The American Revolution had begun.

The Minuteman statue in Concord, Massachusetts.

TIMELINE

1754–1763
The French and Indian War fought primarily between Great Britain and France in North America.

1756–1763
The Seven Years' War fought between Great Britain and its enemies around the world.

SEPTEMBER 1759
British victory at the Battle of Quebec. Most fighting ceases in North America.

OCTOBER 25, 1760
George III becomes the king of Great Britain.

FEBRUARY 10, 1763
The Treaty of Paris formalizes the end of the Seven Years' War.

OCTOBER 7, 1763
Proclamation of 1763 forbids colonists from settling west of the Appalachian Mountains.

APRIL 5, 1764
Sugar Act of 1764.

MARCH 22, 1765
Stamp Act of 1765. Colonists must pay a tax on printed materials.

1767
Townshend Acts of 1767 force colonists to pay a tax on tea and other items.

MARCH 5, 1770
Five American colonists are killed in the Boston Massacre.

DECEMBER 16, 1773
The Boston Tea Party. Chests of tea are destroyed by Boston Patriots to protest the tax on tea.

1774
British Parliament passes the Coercive Acts to punish Boston rebels.

APRIL 19, 1775
The Battles of Lexington and Concord are fought in Massachusetts, west of Boston. The fighting marks the beginning of the American Revolution.

Reenactors portraying British soldiers.

GLOSSARY

ACT

A law or regulation.

BOYCOTT

A refusal to buy something in order to show disapproval.

COLONY

A group of people who settle in a distant territory but remain citizens of their native country.

HOUSE OF BURGESSES

An assembly of elected representatives in Virginia that passed laws and regulations.

MILITIA

Citizens who were part-time soldiers rather than professional army fighters. Militiamen, such as the Minutemen from Massachusetts, usually fought only in their local areas and continued with their normal jobs when they were not needed.

MONOPOLY

Complete control over the production and sales of a product or service.

PARLIAMENT

The law-making body of Great Britain. It consists of the House of Lords and the House of Commons.

PATRIOTS

Colonists who rebelled against Great Britain during the American Revolution.

PLANTATION

A large farm, usually in the Southern Colonies, where crops such as tobacco, sugar cane, rice, or cotton were grown. Workers usually live right on the property. Early plantation owners in North America used cheap slave labor to make their operations more profitable.

RADICALS

Colonists who were strongly opposed to the policies of Great Britain.

REDCOATS

The name that was often given to British soldiers because part of their uniform included a bright red coat.

REVOLUTION

A sudden, sweeping change in government.

SMUGGLE

To bring into or take out of a country secretly without paying fees.

SONS OF LIBERTY

A group of Patriot colonists who banded together to oppose the Stamp Act, Townshend Acts, and other oppressive laws imposed by Great Britain.

TORIES

American colonists who supported Great Britain during the American Revolution. Also called "loyalists."

INDEX